Why the

"New World Order"

will fail

by

Marc Gielissen

Available from the same author;

"Roots in the Congo"

ISBN-13: 978-1974609475

Table of Contents

Acknowledgment

This book reveals some shocking accounts regarding the Vatican, different international organizations, banks and Secret Societies. I am not blaming individuals that are working for or are part of the above mentioned organizations, only their leaders.

When I talk about the elite, I am not necessarily referring to all wealthy people, but rather to those who are using their money and power to control other people.

A special appreciation and thanks goes to my editor C. Johnson who made it possible to reach a very tight publication deadline.

Introduction

I wrote this book as a guidance for people searching some answers to what is happening around us. The knowledge that I will share is based on a combination of years of own research, personal experience and spiritual guidance. It will connect the dots between the New World Order, the approach of the Nibiru system and the awakening of our spirituality.

As the world is close to a total collapse, both socially and economically, the time is right to give another perspective to what will happen soon and most importantly, what we can do to alter our destiny.

"Two things are infinite: the universe and human stupidity; and I'm not sure about the universe."

Albert Einstein

Definition of the "New World Order"

Many official media sources only considered the idea of the creation of a secret New World Order a conspiracy theory. This is largely because it was supported and spread by right wing populists and a handful revolting Anarchists. They claimed that a totalitarian world government would replace the existing sovereign nation states, a thesis that was not taken seriously and therefore characterized as a conspiracy theory.

In recent years; however, as more evidence emerged through information disclosed by remorseful insiders, the so called conspiracy theory turned into reality. It is largely accepted today that the architects of globalization, a secretive power elite have a clear agenda aiming at the creation of a New World Order.

In order to achieve a world domination they (elite) created a net of front organizations that allows them to orchestrate and manipulate major financial as well as political events. Interfering with elections and using political puppets on a worldwide scale is common practice to achieve their objectives.

The political interference will influence financial markets, giving them full control. According to Wikipedia; the term "New World Order", has often been used by 20th century politicians in regards to the balance of power which they were seeking after World War I and World War II. It was Winston Churchill; one of the most famous politicians to have used the term in the past.

The two World Wars (created and financed by the elite), would lead to the creation of the UN (United Nations). It was created in 1945 by US (United States bankers). Then in April 1949 NATO (North Atlantic Treaty Organization) was created by 12 nations. Their objective was to coordinate military defenses against possible Soviet aggression at the time. It all seemed logical and in favor of a mechanism that would keep peace and stability during that period. In retrospective; they were the building blocks of a carefully premeditated plan for world domination rather than peace.

It was the John Birch Society that first pointed out in the 1960s that a cabal (secret plot), composed by greedy bankers and corrupt politicians were trying to use the UN as a foundation to create a "One World Government." The creation of the Federal Reserve in 1913 by private bankers was the historical start of many troubles we experience today. The American writer **Mary M. Davison** in her book; "*The Profound Revolution*", pointed out that there was a direct link between the founders of the Federal Reserve and their desire to create a "New World Order." This organization would give them total control over world politics, finance and last but not least religion.

Another American writer, **Pat Robertson** went even further in his book "*The New World Order*", when he stated that Wall Street, the Federal Reserve, the Council on Foreign

Relations, the Bilderberg group and the Trilateral Commission are pushing into the direction of a " One World Government " , an organization that will serve the Antichrist.

It might look extreme to many readers, but when an organization becomes able to finance wars with the sole objective of creating wealth, there is no other description than it being evil.

The cause of evil

Throughout history, people on Earth are known to be both violent and eager to control and dominate. Religion was an ideal tool for those seeking to control the masses and therefore widely used in order to conquer and submit millions of people around the world into a religion to which they often didn't adhere. The evangelization of Africa, South and Central America are good examples of how people were controlled under disguise of spreading the word of God. In reality they were plundering the countries and enslaving the people to serve their upcoming industries. In my first book *"Roots in the Congo"*, this topic is largely discussed. I share my personal experience of examples of how they used religion to obtain natural resources in order to create wealth. The main question here is, which God would have allowed this?

Don't be mistaken, believing in God or the One Divine Source has nothing to do with religion. Religion is only a man made instrument to control and subordinate different groups of people around the world. We can therefore; assume that this is the reason why church leaders are in cohesion with political leaders. They formed a controlling team to enslave people into a system which they created together. It's a highly efficient and deceiving system that unfortunately only benefits the elite or Illuminati along with some of their direct subordinates and political "puppets."

Major industries that belong to the elite group are also part of this global deceiving system. The companies involved are designed and guided to let people believe that their well being depends on the accumulation of material possessions. In order to increase profitability and production year after year, banks will be used to lend the consumers the money at high interest rates. The money they offer them is made out of thin air and the majority is simply virtual. It's nothing more then a figure on a computer screen. It doesn't physically exist and therefore; it can't have a value yet banks are charging you interest on it. Did you ever wonder if that practice is fair and who is benefiting of your hard work?

This brings us to the Federal Reserve, mentioned previously in this book. It is a private organization which is owned by only a handful of people. Some people may call them the Illuminati, let's just call them the elite. This organization is functioning completely independent from any governmental control and able to act as it wishes. It is therefore; rather the Federal Reserve that has control over them, using the distorted power of money as they provide loans to the Government. The harsh reality being that many countries are bankrupt because they are so indebted that they have difficulties to even reimburse the interest. This is precisely what gives them an undeniable absolute power!

The elite's roots are spread within many groups and organizations around the world. They control politics, industries, religions, secret societies such as the Freemasons and the so needed financial markets.

The American sociologist **C. Wright Mills** mentioned in his book *"The Power Elite"* that; *"those political, economic, and military circles which as an intricate set of overlapping small but dominant groups share decisions having at least national consequences. Insofar as national events are decided, the power elite are those who decide them."* His work was written in 1957. Since that time the structure of the elite became leaner and less people became part of it. Today the Vatican and a handful of extremely wealthy bankers have total control of the Federal Reserve and use the organization to achieve their dark objectives.

The elite have the power to start or end wars at will just for profit. They are the people working towards a New World Order, an organization that will contain a one world religion, one world currency and a one world government. The structure will make it so much easier to control and enslave the world's population in order to implement their egocentric ideology.

The IMF (International Monetary Fund), World Bank, UN (United Nations), WTO (World Trade Organization), and many other international organizations are all part of this global structure and the basis of the new world order. It has been in creation for a very long time and it's extremely close to implementation today.

In a very subtle way they convince the public opinion that their organizations (mentioned above), are developing and by definition helping Third World countries in need. The World Bank is an interesting example; as it provides loans for often unproductive projects, such as bridges in the middle of a jungle (where there is no traffic), or the construction of roads that only lead to the factories owned by the elite. Many projects are not contributing to the poor indigenous population in their struggle to survive.

An interesting example; was the construction of the main road from Kinshasa to Matadi in the DR Congo, where a contract of the World Bank was allocated to a Chinese company, which used their own laborers (Chinese prisoners), rather than to employ local people to do the work. It is clear that many projects are rather meant to please regional politicians and multinational Corporations, all part of a widespread organization implementing the New World Order.

The initial goals of the World Bank are clear; end extreme poverty and boost what they call *"shared prosperity."* Unfortunately, none of the above noble objectives are realized today. As a former business leader and having been actively involved in different developing countries projects', I am a first hand witness of the above. I certainly agree that they created and still create a great amount of prosperity. However; I definitely disagree that this is shared with the people. As far as I can judge from personal experience on the ground, living conditions for millions of people have deteriorated over the years.

Even in their communication to the world they are deceiving us by false or distorted information. The World Bank's "shared prosperity" indicator, which is showing that poor countries are doing better after a WB intervention, is a fundamental and incorrect vision presented to the world. The reality instead, is that only a few people within the country became richer (much richer), not the population, leaving an extreme inequality versus shared prosperity in the country.

Before providing a loan, the (WB) organization is well aware of the fact that those poor countries will never be able to reimburse their debts, not even the interest they charge on the loan. The ultimate hidden goal here, is to leave poor countries open to a foreign (private – elite) control of their often precious natural resources, or even an option to simply privatize state owned organizations, leaving them very vulnerable.

The DR Congo is a very good example of how the rich mineral resources are only benefiting a handful of people, all connected to their masters (The elite). Since the end of the colonial period there has been no sign of any improvement in the living conditions of the population, which leaves them even more vulnerable to work for the elite in often despicable conditions. It became the accepted slavery of the 21ˢᵗ Century. Unfortunately, a destiny shared by all people that will be forced to work for the elite during the end times of the New World Order. If you think that it will only happen to people in Africa, or in any other developing regions, think twice.

When **Nikola Tesla** (1856 – 1943), found a way to use Earth's electromagnetic field to produce and deliver free electricity to the community, he was brutally stopped by the elite. They destroyed his laboratory and already operational equipment. It became clear to the elite that if Tesla would succeed in his venture, they wouldn't be able to make any profit. It became a turning point in our industrial future and most likely a missed opportunity to live in a more spiritual world where money and profit would have been less important.

Tesla worked intuitively with nature's forces and found an extraordinary power from within to discover them. In his book; "My inventions: The autobiography of Nikola Tesla" he wrote that; "*Most persons are so absorbed in the contemplation of the outside world that they are wholly oblivious to what is passing on within themselves."*

Rather than using the freely available electromagnetic energy, the elite preferred to focus on the use of oil and coal as basis for the new industry. Unfortunately, this would be the start of a not instantly perceived, but real enslavement of the masses. The greed of the elite and their thirst for control and power only increased over the years, turning our society into a materialistic egocentric world.

Due to the fact that the elite are also controlling the media, only information that serves their cause will be transmitted to the public, using TV, written press, movies, and even the Internet today. They won't hesitate to discredit a specific country's leader because he or she doesn't comply with their policy (often resulting in an assassination or coup), or to create diversions in order to hide the real agenda. Deception is the rule, not an exception in their media approach.

They have several proven techniques and the right people to implement them in order to create wars, destabilize financial markets and influence the so called "democratic elections" around the world. This is all at will, just to give the reader an idea of how powerful this organization is. The top of the elite are often linked to the practice of satanic rituals and worship. I will refrain from citing different names in this publication, but most of you will know them very well, as they are high profile people. We will dig a bit deeper into this aspect later.

From a psychological perspective; we should try to understand why people become monsters and commit horrible crimes, such as the holocaust during World War II, or more recently the genocide in Rwanda and the ongoing most atrocious violence generated by ISIS, just to mention a few. Are the people committing those crimes born evil? The answer to that question is NO.

Stanley Milgram (1963), stated in his research paper on obedience and authority, in which he questioned the fact why millions of innocent people were systematically killed on command between 1933 and 1945, that the commands *"originated in the mind of a single person, but they could only be carried out on a massive scale if a very large number of persons obeyed orders."*

According to Milgram's thesis; evil is not something that is ingrained, even good people can become evil minded due to the circumstances in which they live,   people they meet or associate with, or leaders they value and respect.   When people are trusting and following a leader, they will execute his or her commands, focusing on getting their part of the job done as best as they can, leaving moral judgment to the leader, and by doing so, they won't feel any remorse of their acts. Milgram's study could therefore explain why peaceful people turn violent.

The above described phenomenon is happening to many young people recruited by ISIS today. In a much broader perspective, the leaders of the New World Order are doing exactly the same, hence the reason why many people are not really aware (or care) about the real agenda. Many industry leaders are following the global idea (ingrained by the elite), of a materialistic world, only focusing on making profit by indoctrinating the idea that consumers need the products they produce, rather than improve the wellbeing of our society.

The objective of the elite is to integrate a "poverty consciousness" into the minds of our global materialistic minds, forcing individuals into a constant pressure to gain material possessions and by doing so, creating a feeling of increased personal power, security and status. In a very clever way, the elite managed to social engineer a fear of poverty and feeling of being a less respected person if not actively and successfully part of the global consumerism economy.

The sole objective of our current materialistic world is to breed narcissistic personalities with no empathy for other people.

An egocentric world where people are equating values on accumulated wealth and the direct resulting thought of self esteem and obtained status. External wealth will therefore; become the benchmark to evaluate and define a person's achievements and value in this world.

We are deceived again by being forced to think that materialism is the only true nature of reality and that there is nothing else behind matter. They don't want us to become spiritual and compassionate...love will destroy their business!!

Agenda of the New World Order

The order of the Illuminati was created in 1776 by university professor Adam Weishaupt in Upper-Bavaria (Germany). He recruited his followers from German Masonic lodges and was teaching rationalism through mystery schools. He built up his organization as a strictly hierarchical structure, in line with the one of the Society of Jesus (Jesuit). Although he left the church when he was young, he reconciled before his death. The occult organization was created on the request of Mayer Amshel Rothschild. Many researchers agree on the fact that his organization is considered as the base of the current elite and founding fathers of the New World Order.

Although there are many contradictions in the role played by the Vatican, there is evidence that the Illuminati infiltrated the Vatican. The author **Piers Compton** mentioned in his book, *"The Broken Cross"*, that in his research he found traces that the all-seeing eye in the triangle symbol was used by leading Catholics and more specifically by Jesuits. You can find it on stamps of the Vatican issued in 1978 and furthermore; according to Compton, Pope John XXII wore the symbol of the all-seeing eye in the triangle on his personal cross.

He also claimed that several hundred leading Catholic priests, bishops and cardinals are member of secret societies and that it is widely believed that Pope John Paul II was a member of the Illuminati despite the fact that he approved the 1983 Declaration on Masonic Association from the Congregation of the Doctrine of the Faith, reiterating the church's objections to Freemasonry. In this book you will find out more about the Vatican and their often dual face to the world, showing a schizophrenic evil.

What we know with certainty is that many Catholics joined the Masonic organization to benefit from a number of social services not provided by other organizations. Even within the church the answers and own laws are often presented in a twilight zone, leaving space for speculation. The church itself being a secretive organization, is not making it easier to discover the truth. Many of the circulating stories are therefore; based on assumptions. They are often misunderstood readings or twisted from reality.

According to *socioecohistory.wordpress.com;* the Council of 13 or the Grand Druid Council, represents the sixth and therefore highest level of witchcraft. They're said to be an element of the hidden Satanic hierarchy government in close cooperation with the order of the Jesuits. Many research documents are pointing to a close historical link between the Illuminati and the Jesuits (established by Pope Paul III in 1540). This was originally used to counter reformation movements in Europe, resulting; in a loss of both political and religious power to the Vatican. The Jesuits are known as a geo-political organization, structured as a secret military operation. The Superior General or "Black Pope" (he dresses in black and stands in the shadow of the white Pope), is the real force behind the Vatican.

The Illuminati or elite organization have their roots in Egyptian/Babylonian religions in which the secular class reports to the priestly class, who are in direct contact with the Gods. It is said that the Council of 13 belongs to that priestly class and report to the Triumvirate (Told to be Satanic Rothschild bloodlines). The latter will then communicate with demons, fallen angels or Satan directly.

The so called Committee of 300 belong to the profane class which handle politics (the actual world government). Many researchers on the subject are convinced that the power behind the Illuminati are fallen angels and not human. I could not find supporting evidence for this claim, so I leave the interpretation open to the reader.

The New World Order has often be described as just another conspiracy theory, but recent actions and feedback from inside whistleblowers are clearly indicating that it is a real threat to humanity. When a secretive elite takes over control of banks, Governments, economies and define warfare as well as financial markets, there is no doubt that they have a well prepared agenda. This evil plan has been in the making for a very long time and is ready to be implemented today.

The elite is not working alone to achieve their objectives and many known and lesser known organizations are part of the global system to gain a total control. There's evidence that the Vatican plays an important or even a leading role. If we look into our past, this shouldn't be a surprise, just look at how the church controlled a major part of the world through religion.

The church leaders aren't as saint as they are depicted today is beyond any doubt. There is enough evidence available today to prove that Pope Pius XII had an agreement with Hitler, a person he admired. The treaty was based on the Vatican's 1929 agreement with Mussolini. Pope Pius XII never made a public condemnation of the Holocaust. He allowed the church to profit from goods taken from the victims of the Nazis. Which god are they representing?

According to *bibliotecapleyades.net;* and different other research documents, the Vatican together with the Military Order of Malta has control over:

- NATO

- The European Commission

- The United Nations

- Different Central Banks around the world

- Council of Foreign Affairs

- Multinational Corporations

- Secret Service

- A large number of societies and cults, including the Freemasons and Opus Dei

Dr. Stephen D. Mumford also argued in his book; *"American Democracy and The Vatican: Population Growth and National Security"* that ; *"the Vatican controls governments, completely or partially."* He further revealed an intense struggle within the church itself, as the structure doesn't allow any internal opposition against any position taken by the Pope.

Professor of Sociology at the University of Montreal **Jean-Guy Vaillancourt**, who is a Catholic and the author of *"Papal Power; a study of Vatican Control over Lay Catholic elites"*, explains in his extensive study about the efforts of the Vatican to achieve power that *"The Vatican is, above all, an organizational weapon in the hands of the papacy and top ecclesiastical officials."* He mentioned that the Vatican was not only a religious, but more so an economical and political power house searching for total control.

The resistance of the masses is not a priority targeting wealthy people, but rather against how an elite group is concocting plans to control them, by creating a system to which they can't escape and in which every form of freedom is eradicated.

Any secret society is by definition suspicious in its objectives and therefore; not in line with the oneness the world desperately needs today. The opposition of the people who are waking up, is therefore; perfectly in line with the laws of the universe. It will be presented as stigmatized knowledge, but don't be mistaken, their actions are clear. There is more than sufficient evidence to assume that the plan initiated by the Council of 13 is being implemented today.

How subtle the elite communicates becomes clear in former President George H.W. Bush's speech (*Towards a New World Order*), on **September 11, 1990,** during a joint session of the US Congress when he stated the following;

"Until now, the world we've known has been a world divided – a world of barbed wire and concrete block, conflict and war. Now, we can see a new world coming into view. A world in which there is the very real prospect of a "new world order." In the words of Winston Churchill, a "world order" in which "the principles of justice and fair

play...protect the weak against the strong..." A world where the United Nations, freed from cold war stalemate, is poised to fulfill the historic vision of its founders. A world in which freedom and respect for human rights find a home among all nations."

Although the objectives in his speech are noble, the reality on the field today is rather deceiving. We are closer than ever to a new World War. Disorder and political chaos are the norm, even our most fundamental rights and pursuit of happiness are under assault. Their motto is rather *"Ordo – ab – Chaos"* , or order out of chaos. When there is chaos it becomes easy to install forced order.

These are some of the important principles of the New World Order:

- One world Army
- One Religion
- One world Government
- One elected world Parliament
- One world Tribunal
- One world Police force
- One world Currency

The question we should ask ourselves is; who will benefit out of this One World Order, and will it bring us a better society? The reader probably knows the answers already, certainly not a society based on love and compassion, but rather on materialism and egocentrism.

Author **Paul Watson** stated in his book; *"Order out of Chaos – Elite Sponsored Terrorism & the New World Order"* that *"it is the biggest threat humanity has ever faced. Moreover, it is a menace to each and everyone of us individually."* This is the reason why we should be vigilant and aware of what is happening before it's too late.

In sharp contrast to the above New World Order puppets, I would like to cite President **John F. Kennedy's** speech on April 27, 1961 , when he said that;

" The very word secrecy is repugnant, in a free and open society. For we are, as people, inherently and historically opposed to secret societies, to secret proceedings and to secret oaths.

For we are opposed around the world by monolithic and ruthless conspiracy that relies primarily on covert means for expanding its sphere of influence – on infiltration instead of invasion, on subversion instead of elections, on intimidation instead of free choice, on guerrillas by night instead of armies by day.

It is a system which has conscripted vast human and material resources into the building of a tightly knit, highly efficient machine that combines military, diplomatic, intelligence, economic, scientific and political operations. Its preparations are concealed, not published. Its mistakes are buried not headlined.

Its dissenters are silenced, not praised. No expenditure is questioned, no rumor is printed, no secret is revealed."

President John F. Kennedy was murdered on November 22, 1963.

It is a fact; that one of his last executive orders was to provide debt free money for America, refusing to pay interest to the private City of London foreign bankers (Rothschild). President Kennedy wanted to get rid of the unconstitutional Federal Reserve and this unfortunately, costed him his life.

This brings us back to the use of widespread influence and power by the elite in order to achieve their objectives.

What is happening to our Earth?

According to many independent, both current and ancient researchers, there is a planetary system approaching Earth. As we live in a binary star system, this is a natural event. This planetary system consists of our own sun's twin, which is called Nemesis, it's a brown dwarf star. Nemesis is difficult to detect, even using infrared, because it is surrounded by dust clouds of iron oxide. What researchers found up to now is that Nemesis has at least three planets revolving it. They are Nibiru and Helion, both with their own moons, and the third one being Arboda.

In 1940, a Chilean astronomer **Carlos Munoz Ferrada**, predicted already that governments around the world would attempt to cover up the arrival of the above mentioned system. He referred to Nibiru or planet x as a comet-planet, because its size is similar to that of planets, but it's speed and elliptical orbit are similar to that of a comet. He called it Hercolubus and studied it for almost 59 years of his life. Ferrada was able to specify the mass, velocity, orbital time and its trajectory.

The Sumerian tablets gave us more substantial evidence of the existence of the approaching system when archaeologist and writer **Zecharia Sitchin** deciphered the tablets and described his findings in great detail in his book *"the 12th planet."* He came with overwhelming scientific proof of the fact that this event takes place every 3600 years.

The Sumerians lived about 6000 years ago in a region which is currently known as Iraq. It is not this author's objective to go into details and repeat what a multitude of other authors have already communicated. For the skeptics or interested in a detailed feedback among you, I would recommend to read his book. The planet that is referred to as Planet X or Nibiru is already in our solar system and approaching Earth. There is great amount of information as well as disinformation available on the Internet and in written articles today. In the end, it is up to the reader to do some own research and find a personal perspective and believe. My only advice is not to use official organizations like NASA to get answers because they will deceive you, which could be to avoid a general panic, to protect the elite, or maybe a combination of both.

NASA always gave conflicting information, first confirming its existence in the 80s and later denying the same. More recently **Jim Green** (director of NASA's planetary science division), said that it was too early to say with certainty that there is a Planet Nibiru, or Planet 9 as they call it. In the same message however; they mention that Caltech researchers found an object with a mass 10 times that of Earth and is in orbit on an elliptical course.

It is evident that NASA doesn't want to disclose it, but they are facing millions of people already seeing the objects, as the system becomes visible in the sky today. The internet is flooded with pictures of the incoming system.

They have no other choice then to slowly release information in order not to be completely ridiculed.

When the archaeologist and writer Zecharia Sitchin interviewed the supervising astronomer of the US Naval Observatory Robert S.Harrington in 1990 (the man who discovered Nibiru after Carlos Munoz Ferrada), it was clear that he was absolutely confident about his findings. He even set up a special telescopic observatory in New Zealand to track it. There is still a mystery around his sudden death in 1993, people close to him suggested that he was killed.

Harrington was not the only person to have supported the existence of Nibiru, also Ray T. Reynolds, a NASA scientist proclaimed its existence in 1992. Lately, NASA is trying to spread disinformation about the event in order to protect the New World Order plans of the elite.

As the system is in our solar system, following its elliptical course, it will interfere with all the planets within our solar system, including our own sun. During the approach we experience an increase in Earthquakes and strange weather phenomenon, already happening around the world now. When the system will be close enough to Earth in order to pull our magnetic field, it could ultimately trigger a pole shift.

According to what is called the tribulation (in the Bible mentioned as a period in which God will judge), which is the 7 year it will take the Nibiru system to leave our inner solar system, our Earth will experience a period of great devastation. Many ancient scriptures also associate this time period with the advent of the Antichrist, as God will remove the church (called the Rapture).

The period of tribulation is divided in two parts of three and a half years. The first three and a half years are called the lesser tribulation as the Antichrist will be in disguise, showing himself as a "good person", willing to help humanity, whereas in the last three and a half years, or the great tribulation, he will be publicly recognized and worshiped.

There are many groups on Facebook, as well as other public media platforms, which are researching and independently reporting events around the world that are not covered by the traditional media. Their objective is to inform as many people as possible and create awareness of what is coming our way. With a possible pole shift looming, there are well organized survival groups active today.

One of the groups I would recommend for detailed scientific independent information on an almost daily basis is "*Hidden Knowledge – unravelling the pole shift*", a group created by **Mark Elkin,** who is also the force behind a survival group in the UK called "New Earth."

The American writer **David Meade** mentioned in this book "*Will Planet X signal the rapture*", that the danger of a cataclysmic event is imminent and based on his findings on religious scriptures, such as the Bible and The Book of Revelation.

Could this be the reason why the Vatican invested millions of dollars to build their own observatory in southern Arizona? David Meade also mentioned that *"the Vatican in Rome regards Planet X as the prophesied and much dreaded "Wormwood" of revelation 8:10-11."*

The reader will find a multitude of possible dates for the fly by of the inbound system, however; I personally believe that we will have to wait and observe what will happen. There will be clear signs to give humanity a final warning. There are well organized private (not governmental) groups of people keeping an eye on our skies, as well as the Earth itself (as mentioned before). As we all know, time in space terms is quite different to what we perceive here on Earth. Some independent researchers follow the interpretation of the book of revelations to the letter and believe that the event will take place on September 23, 2017. Author David Meade (mentioned before), is one of the advocates of this assumption.

However; according to recent deciphering of the Nostradamus predictions, it would only be in the year 2040 that the Earth will go through the first cataclysm, the second and final one being in 2046. It is **Jason M. Breashears** in his book *"Nostradamus and the planets of apocalypse"*, that refers to the system of isometric projections to predict future events based on past events. He could describe a multitude of events very accurately predicted in the past, giving his theory at least some credibility.

What we know with certainty at this point in time, is that it will happen in line with what many other civilizations before us showed and predicted in so many different ways. Ignoring their messages and warnings would not only be a mistake, but also show disrespect for higher civilizations then our own. It is not because we live today that we are the highest intelligence that ever walked this Earth. There is overwhelming evidence of the existence of much higher civilizations than ours today.

Evil forces, which were extensively described in the bible, as well as in many other religious scriptures are showing their real face today. Slowly but surely people start understanding what is going on and why our world is based on materialism, greed and not love as it should be.

The arrival of Nibiru in our solar system triggered a spiritual awakening of many (not all) people on this Earth, allowing them to see evil that was invisible for them before. It is not this writer's intention to search for any logical or scientific explanation for this, as it is far beyond our current comprehension, although we could make some assumptions.

The most important and interesting phenomenon is the fact; that we start seeing what is happening around us, whereas before we were completely blind, following like sheep, regardless of the consequences. This is also the main reason why so many people around the world are revolting against the church today (look at the recent claims of pedophilia), something that would have been unimaginable just 20 years ago. There's a growing revolt against governments and their institutions (many political leaders are disgraced and judged for their actions today). People start being aware of the fact that distorted information is coming from the media and are questioning many other events happening around us, this phenomenon is called the awakening.

Slowly our civilization is changing from a materialistic to a spiritual society, where love and respect for each other will open another dimension, something we never experienced before. As the Nibiru system approaches Earth, people will start changing at an incredible speed. Some will become restless and violent, because they are spiritually not ready to enter this new dimension and experience it as a threat, others become more enlightened. People that can't cope with it will be left behind in our current dimension. There is nothing bad or wrong about it, they just need more time, but they missed this train.

After being enslaved by evil forces since a very long time, humanity finally has an opportunity to free itself and enter that new dimension where love and peace reign over power and materialism. In order to keep a total control; the elite will use all means, making it harder for people to escape from their atrocious plan. The forces of evil around us will do anything to keep us in their grip, because they need us as the slaves of their materialistic and consumerist world.

We cannot just blame them, we are all born with a free will and most of us followed the greedy and material world route.

As long as we believe that matter (as defined in materialism), is the fundamental substance in nature, and that all things in our consciousness are the sole result of material interactions, we are still materialists. It is only when we understand that all matter is created in the mind first, giving humans powers they lost since a very long time, that we will discover spirituality.

Researchers are continually finding more evidence that our brain has the power to change the body's physiology, which would give us the ability to self-heal damaged cells, just by influencing them by our thoughts. The law of mentalism, one of the most important laws of the universe, will explain how this happens (see chapter The laws of the universe).

What to expect from the elite?

Being well aware of the spiritual changes which are driving more and more people into alternative ways of living, by turning their backs to the current establishment, they will need to block all escape routes when declaring marshal law based on events they will initiate or provoke. We will cover some of the possibilities in order for them to achieve this state of emergency later in this book.

It means that they will force people into a totalitarian regime, their so called "New World Order." In order to achieve that objective, freedom will have to be restricted to an absolute minimum. Conditions of fear will be ingrained via the media in a very subtle and gradual way.

The creation and financing of ISIS is a good recent example of how the elite work. Using the media they justify actions and reduce the liberty of citizens at the same time. Carefully planning attacks in different big cities to increase fear and insecurity in order to enable them to intervene, using drastic actions, which will end all individual freedom in the name of 'security' and the so called 'terrorist threat.'

They count on unstable brainwashed, trained and already criminal individuals to increase the number of attacks. It is not that complicated to brainwash people that are already ingrained with idealistic and radical religious views. Killing in name of Allah and using the Islam religion is just another example of how people can be radicalized by their beliefs. Never underestimate the power of religion.

Today we see cameras on many public places, electronic surveillance of everyone's moves, our phones and computers are under their control and scanned on a regular basis. Are you aware of the fact that by law all your phone calls are registered and saved for at least 6 months by your telecom operators? They know exactly what we do, with whom we are, where we are, what books we read, which movies we watch, our fields of interest, both religious and political views and the list goes on. Money becomes more and more virtual, very soon the use of cash will be prohibited completely, giving them full electronic control over our spending.

Our credit cards are monitored all the time, they know exactly where and for what we spent our money. If you refuse to comply to the system they will impose, it will only be a click on a computer keyboard to block your account, leaving you without any financial means to live. As they progress in the implementation of their plans, we will all become prisoners of the system.

In order to have full control over the masses, they need to increase the power game and therefore create the right conditions to realize that objective. This can only be realized by creating chaos on a worldwide scale. This is done by creating conflicts, war, and even natural catastrophes which are initiated by new technologies using geoengineering and HAARP (High Frequency Active Auroral Research Program), the new secret weapon used for weather modification and electromagnetic warfare.

According to Wikipedia, it is funded by the US Navy, the US Air Force, the University of Alaska Fairbanks and the Defense Advanced Research Projects Agency (DARPA). Although scientists claim they have no ability to weaponize the weather and that their objectives are only to study the basic natural processes in our ionosphere (our uppermost part of the atmosphere), under influence of solar interaction and how this affects radio signals.

Despite the Government's version, many independent researchers are convinced they have the ability to control weather. **Michael Chossudovsky** who is a Professor at the University of Ottawa (Canada) stated in his book *"America War on Terrorists"* that; "recent scientific evidence suggests that HAARP is fully operational and has the capability of triggering floods, hurricanes, droughts and earthquakes." According to an article in globalresearch.ca, physicist **Dr. Bernard Eastlund** claims that HAARP is *"the largest ionosphere heater ever built."* The same source mentioned that it was presented as a research program for the US Air Force, but disclosed military documents reveal that its real purpose is to induce ionosphere modifications in order to alter weather patterns and the ability to disrupt radar and communication on a global scale.

According to **Rosalie Bertell** (President of the international institute of Concern for Public Health), the use of HAARP can disrupt our ionosphere. It will not only create holes, but long incisions in the protective layer that should protect earth from deadly radiation. The ability of controlling weather, earthquakes and floods gives them the power to create the right circumstances in order to lead to the instigation of a martial law, bringing a halt to all liberty and chances for people to escape the system. It is clear that the ability to use 'climate warfare' is a real threat to humanity. This power will play a major role in the creation of the New World Order.

By creating a one world order they will not only have control over your life, but also over your beliefs. There are already several indicators pointing to the fact that a one world religion will be created; unfortunately, people will be tricked again into worshipping anything but God. It is thought that the elite receive their power directly from dark forces, who worked their way up over many years, to create the world in which we live today.

Despite all the negative elements mentioned above, we are at the end of a period in which evil ruled this world and many of us are ready to move into the new era. Any form of change; as often, will create resistance, that's why it won't be easy, there will be a fearsome fight to hold on to the power they have been developing for such a long time.

This is a battle between forces that are far beyond our comprehension, but we are all very much involved in it, both physically and mentally. Many people are focused on the physical changes that are damaging our Earth during the passing of the Nibiru system, which is quite normal, as they also fear for their physical body (life). I would like to point out to the reader that regardless of the destruction or rather cleansing of our Earth, the spiritual change will be the most important one, that is the main reason I was told to write this book.

I am neither a prophet, clairvoyant or sensation seeker. During and after my long ocean passages I received so many spiritual important messages, that they completely altered my life and its purpose. I worked very closely with the elite before I decided to abandon a highly paid and respected job, a decision that was taken in a split second of spiritual awakening. A fact that still intrigues me up to this day. I know very well how they function, what their objectives are and what thrives them.

It doesn't mean that the people working for them are necessarily all bad or evil. Many among them are not even aware of their ultimate evil plans and can therefore function well in that environment. I did too; until I realized that there was something fundamentally wrong, not only to what I was doing, but to the system, the organization and the world in which we live. It would be the beginning of a very long search.

Materialism is deeply ingrained in our world, it became the new God. Having money became synonym of being successful and by consequence happy and respected. The reality however; is that if we look around us, we see only few happy people, because most are just unable to reach society's benchmark.

We live in a world where consumption is king and the marketers are doing a wonderful job in convincing people that they really need what the industry is producing. The banks are just waiting for you to lend their virtual money so that they can charge you high interests rates. This economical system will allow the industries to increase production in order to enrich them and most of all, gain power over the consumer. They are in some strange way addicted to their products, giving them a false impression of happiness. This is the very subtle way in which the elite slowly but surely enslave the population, using the beautiful disguise of increasing the living standards.

Advance in technology is only an advantage if it serves the people. Unfortunately, most of our current technology doesn't really benefit humanity. Even our smartphones which are giving us so much pleasure are taking our freedom away. They not only disclose all our activities, they are not benefiting our normal social interaction. We don't talk with each other any longer, we only text. The real objective of the elite is to enrich only a few of their subordinates and enslave the majority. We have less multinational Corporations than ever before and their numbers are decreasing rapidly, they merge or disappear, leaving the consumers no choice of alternative supplier and as such vulnerable to poor quality products at higher prices. This is exactly what the globalists want.

It is perfectly possible to build high quality products that last a lifetime however, that would be against the current planned consumption system in which products have to fail only after a few years. The new and much loved policy of industries is called 'Planned obsolescence' where the life span of the product is artificially limited after a well defined period of time. The only objective is to reduce time between purchases, which will increase the long-term sales volume. The machines have to keep running, production always has to increase, regardless of the fact if people want, need or even can afford the produced products. If you can't afford it, banks will lend you the money, enslaving you even more!

The above examples are all part of our current society, a society that is about to experience a major change. The reader will understand that drastic measures are necessary to change what has been going wrong for such a long time. We arrived at that crucial turning point in the evolution of our world, a point that has been described in many ancient holy scriptures of different religions and advanced civilization before us. It has been seen by Nostradamus, Edgar Casey and many others. The question is not if it will happen, but rather when.

There is sufficient evidence to assume that the only plan of the elite is to create a world government that will be ruled by them. This won't stop there, they will do everything in their power to avoid non initiated people to acquire the necessary knowledge of the laws of the universe and empower humanity to move into a new dimension, a place where they would lose all their power.

Unfortunately for the elite, many people are intuitively pushed to increase their frequency, and by doing so, they are also influencing the global consciousness into a higher frequency.

Our connection with alien races

There is more than enough convincing evidence available today that ancient alien civilizations played a very important role on Earth, much more than we can imagine. Most of the evidence is probably on the bottom of our oceans, but Archaeologists found sufficient direct evidence in the Sumerian tablets that clearly mention the existence of Nibiru (part of the recently discovered solar system on an unconventional elliptic course), and the landing of the Anunnaki on Earth with an interval of 3600 years. The time frame in which the Nibiru system comes close to Earth, before returning on its course out of our inner solar system.

The Anunnaki were referred to as *"Those who from heaven came to Earth"* by the Sumerians. It is not this author's intention to elaborate on the subject, but it is necessary to have the basic information in order to understand the next part of the book. The human race as we know it today is believed to be a product of the Anunnaki. This doesn't mean that there is no God !

It was the controversial Swiss author **Erich von Daniken** who projected the idea in his best seller of 1968; *"Chariots of the Gods?"*, that we had an important extraterrestrial influence and were visited by "ancient astronauts." Although he was certainly not the first to advance this idea, but rather the first who made the idea popular to a large audience.

As with humans, there are a multitude of different alien races, of which some are good and others are bad, quite similar to the differences we experience between humans here on Earth. Those civilizations have always visited us, and according to recent disclosure of official documents, some never left. The elite are in possession of technology that is far beyond our current public knowledge, they are hiding this from us for a very long time.

Some is based on what is called reverse or back engineering, which is seen as a process in which design information and knowledge is used to reproduce the same technology. Another part of the new technology comes directly from aliens who are cooperating with the elite.

An Email released by **WikiLeaks,** revealed that former astronaut Edgar D. Mitchell, wrote to American politician John Podesta, (Ex adviser to President Barack Obama), that the Vatican was aware of the existence of Aliens and their involvement in helping us to understand *"zero point energy."*

In his Email he mentioned *"the urgency as I see it to explain as much as possible to you and President Obama about what we know for sure about our nonviolent ETI from the contiguous universe who are peacefully assisting us with bringing zero point energy to our fragile planet"* (*source WikiLeaks*).

Their concern is the violent nature of humanity and the risks involved of misusing a technology that would open up the possibility of completely free energy from empty space. As with Nikola Tesla before, I am sure that the technology, if shared, will only be used to control the population, not to benefit it. Mitchel also claimed that alien life is *"the highest form of intelligence that works directly with God."*

If you see a UFO in the sky, it will not necessarily mean it is of alien origin, so don't be misguided again by false signs in the skies. They will use any means to activate martial law in order to implement the New World Order, even if it would be a fake alien invasion. All this activity is closely monitored by aliens that are here to help us. It all seems straight out of a science fiction series, but unfortunately the reader will see the reality and significance of their actions very soon.

It is not a coincidence that NASA just created a new position for a person whose job will be to help protect the world against alien interference, the strange part however, is why they announce this right now. Governments around the world are well aware of the presence of aliens and the fact that they were here long before we inhabited this planet.

According to different sources, we are close to an official announcement by global governments that intelligent aliens are amongst us, the question remains why they are planning to disclose this right now?

Could the 'Project Blue Beam' conspiracy theory become reality?

This theory suggests that NASA is attempting to implement a New Age religion headed by the Antichrist in order to simulate a second coming in order to help start the New World Order. Another science fiction tale ? I am not so sure.

The Canadian journalist and writer **Serge Monast** (who died in 1996 under suspicious circumstances) mentioned in his book; *"Project Blue Beam (NASA)"* , based on inside information given to him by contrite politicians, military and intelligence persons that felt the necessity to disclose what they thought to be a crime against humanity, that the foundation of the New World Order is the creation of a new global religion, making it the ultimate instrument of their dictatorship.

Monast argued that the first step in the NASA Blue Beam Project is to break down all prior archaeological knowledge, create hoaxed new discoveries with the only purpose to deceive people into new beliefs. It will eradicate all former religious doctrines in order to explain the errors humanity made before in their respective forms of believe. Different recent movies and a variety of media publications are supporting their new findings in order to "prepare" the masses for a radical change in beliefs. The objective is to destroy all beliefs of Christians as well as Muslims by presenting them false proof that all our past religions were wrong.

In order to achieve this, they use technology to create earthquakes on specific locations on Earth, those earthquakes will then be used to discover new archaeological proof that our past interpretation of religion was wrong. The most intriguing part of the project is the projection on our skies (using the sodium layer at about 60 miles) of a simulation of the prophesied end of times scenario.

They will project different Gods in line with local beliefs, Christ for Christians, Allah for Muslims etc. They will speak the local language, even dialect so people can clearly understand them. They will be using very advanced 3 dimensional holograms in the sky. Each God will merge into one single being, it will become the new global God.

The new God will be shown to all nations around the world in order to materialize the one world religion.

The laws of the universe

According to the Kybalion (which is the study of The Hermetic Philosophy of Ancient Egypt and Greece), first published in 1908 under the pseudonym of "the Three Initiates" , and *"The Science of being"* , written by **Baron Eugene Fersen** in 1923, we have seven major universal laws. It is important to understand them in order to know why we are going through this period and what will happen to us, explained in a later phase in this book. Our Universe is governed by seven Universal laws, principles or axioms. All in perfect harmony and balance by virtue of these laws. Within the seven laws we can define three that are immutable (Meaning that they can never be changed) and four that are transitory (They can be transcended or changed).

1 The law of mentalism (Immutable)

All what we see or experience in the physical world has its origin in the mental realm. It is very important to understand the principals, because it shows us that we have a single Universal Consciousness. We could call it the *"Universal mind"* , from where all energy and matter is created. We are all interconnected, every individual's mind is part of the universal mind. Your reality is first created in your mind and then manifested in the material world.

Basic principle: *"All is mind"*

2 The law of correspondence (immutable)

It tells us that; *"as above, so below and as below so above."* There is agreement between the spiritual, physical and mental realms. We are all part of the one source, therefore there is no separation. It is a pattern that exists from the smallest electron to the biggest star and it is not changeable.

The 3 realms being;

- The great Physical realm

- The great Mental realm

- The great Spiritual realm

Basic principle: *"As above, so below:as below, so above"*

3 The law of vibration (Immutable)

Everything is in movement all the time and everything around us vibrates and circles, including our own body. This law tells us that the whole Universe consist of vibration. All things, including we humans, are pure energy and vibrating, although at different frequencies. All our thoughts and emotions are vibrations. When we look at emotions, we know that unconditional love will be the absolute highest and hate the absolute lowest or most dense vibration.

Basic principle: *"Nothing rests, everything moves, vibrates and circles"*

4 The law of polarity (Mutable)

It tells us that everything has its pair of opposites, everything is dual and has poles. Love and hate , positive and negative, energy and matter. People often say that love and hate are close, it's very true as it only takes a person to raise his or her vibration to change hate into love. There are always two sides to everything in the Universe.

Basic principle: *"everything is and isn't at the same time"*

5 The law of rhythm (Mutable)

All things will flow out and flow back in, best to be compared with the swing of a pendulum, where the momentum of right swing will create that of the left swing. We see it in the tides of the sea and even whole civilizations that rise and fall.   Understanding this law will be very important for humanity, as it will help us to bend negative thoughts into positive thoughts and by doing so we create a new reality. It is closely related to the law of polarity.

Basic principle: *"Flow and inflow"*

6 The law of cause and effect (Mutable)

It tells us that every cause has its effect and every effect has his cause. Every single thought, action or even words are created in your mental or inner world, they will set a specific effect in motion that will materialize over time. In my first book *"Roots in the Congo"* , I explained this phenomenon by citing different examples in life were the "power of thought" resulted in the desired outcome.

Basic principle: *"There is no chance, only cause and effect"*

7 The law of gender (Mutable)

Everything has masculine and feminine principles in the Universe. It is present in opposite sexes found in humans, but also in minerals, magnetic poles, electrons etc. It also means that everyone and everything has a masculine and feminine side. For humans this means that in every woman lies the qualities of a man and for any man the qualities of a woman. This is not related to sexuality, only spirituality.

Basic principle: *"Mental gender manifests as feminine and masculine sides in all realms"*

Later on in this publication, we will understand why I elaborated on the laws of the universe and why they are a necessary part of this book. Humanity has made many mistakes in the past, but is on a major crossroad today, ready to change direction. A completely new era, which will change everything we currently experience and know, it will reveal itself to us when the time is right. Humanity will raise the vibrational level in order to enter the new realm of peace and love. A realm or plane in which no more armies will be necessary and people will live by the power of the Universe and the One creator or God.

The spiritual awakening

When a person reaches a state of spiritual awakening, a deep feeling of connection with the divine is experienced. As we learned in the previous chapter about the laws of the Universe, all of this is interconnected. It is exactly that feeling of oneness with nature or the universe that will let us know that we are on a path of enlightenment and ready to increase our frequency.

If we look around us, we will notice that more and more people are turning their back to society as it exists today and choose for a "back to basics" life. Some will buy a boat and sail the seas to escape the mad world. Others will try to live close to nature by building their own self-sustainable life. More people will rely on social media to either report or search for the truth, rather than just watching and absorbing the often twisted truth reported by the media. We'll start questioning different aspects of our life, such as beliefs, habits and ideals we had before. These are all signs of awakening.

Spiritual awakening is happening when the soul is ready for it. As nothing is static and everything moves and evolves, so does our soul. We will see in a later phase why so many people on Earth are suddenly feeling "spiritually awake." Going through the awakening phase is often confusing, even alienating and people experiencing it will often feel lonely or just the opposite, in need for isolation. It's the "letting go of the ego", realizing that our life long striving for money, respect and power were all surrogates for what we perceived as happiness. The real happiness is deep inside and can often be found in the very little things in life. It's the ones we never observed before, this is where we can find true happiness.

Spiritual awakening is not always a smooth ride, it is rather confusing, often created by a feeling that your whole life has been turned upside down and inside out. In the writer's case it led to self-isolation, questioning every part of my former beliefs and values. Other people might experience depression and even chronic anxiety at a certain point, but we all come out of it as reborn with a clear vision of what we want in life. It won't be material wealth, success and power any longer!

Awakening is nothing more than returning to our initial spiritual values from which we were disconnected for such a long time. Our material society doesn't allow for spirituality, as it is too much focused on material success, money and achievements.

Today millions of people around the world realize that despite having success, money and respect, their artificial happiness doesn't fill the void of our soullessness deep inside.

Here are some of the signs that you are awakening:

- You become more sensitive than before

- You experience moments of anxiety and depression

- You start questioning your life's purpose

- A feeling of great change in life

- You start doubting your religious believes

- Fear and uncertainty

- An extreme desire to be alone

- Feeling empathy for others

- Wanting to know the truth

- You become more sensitive

- Vivid dreams

- Some food intolerance

When will the awakening happen?

There are many signs around the world that the masses are awakening. The most important change we noticed recently is that people don't want to live with the lies from politicians any longer. There are rebellions around the world against different regimes and various unlawful practices by the elite. A common feeling of justice is spreading around the world in order to stop injustice and inequality.

We are gaining awareness about the plans of the elite and what their final objectives are. People don't want to be fooled with lies any longer. Remarkably, there is a great synchronicity around the world in what is happening. It's not just a coincidence, but rather connected to the laws of the Universe and as such guided by the invisible hand of God. Everything is falling into place, people are getting organized in a new spirit of awareness. It's all happening at the right time and in the right place. There is a great connection between those who want to change the world and move to that higher frequency.

Isn't the Universe wonderful in the mysterious way it connects events?

A large number of people are returning to spiritual practice in many different ways, but they all have a common connection. Numerous people are using meditation and yoga to achieve an increase in vibration, it is coming to them in a natural way...from within.

New planned events by the elite can no longer be hidden, we are assisted by the Universe and the increase in vibration largely influenced by the approach of the Nibiru solar system. It is enabling many to discover the truth, as there will be no hiding from it any longer. All will become clear for those who open their eyes and enjoy the new spiritual awakening.

We arrived in a phase where Nibiru's system energy is influencing our consciousness. It's one of the most important messages received from my spiritual guide. As we are all part of the universe, we also experience the changes on a spiritual level when the vibrations will increase. Despite all the doom predictions of a looming disaster on a physical level, it will be a huge opportunity for humanity to change the appearance of this world and go into the oneness dimension.

What we need to understand is that the human consciousness is directly connected to the incoming system and therefore our thoughts, emotions and desires will be reflected on an energetic level. In other words, what we project will be returned to us, which is completely in line with the law of mentalism which we discussed before.

We are influencing the incoming system by our thoughts and feelings and in return it will influence us. The mysterious but wonderful universal interaction. The Nibiru system is able to generate enormous amounts of energy, enough to help millions of people into a state of spiritual awakening in a very short period of time. We all know how much we are influenced by celestial objects in the solar system around us. The moon and planets are influencing the tides and even our mood, but the influence of the Nibiru system is significant and is changing us currently today.

It is amplifying our feelings and thoughts in a major way and it is all happening right now. This is one of the main reasons why there's so much violence and frustration around the world. Is it the explanation why we are on the verge of yet another devastating World War? It will only lower our frequencies, something the elite crave for.

Fortunately, at the same time it also works in a positive way by amplifying the feelings of people with a positive mindset. Those of which who send love into the universe. It shows us the polarity between good and bad, yet another law of the Universe.

The event and changes happening right now are so important for the universe and all creatures that are part of it. We are currently supported by Alien civilizations with the only purpose of increasing the vibrational level on Earth in order to ascent into a new era. Pulling Earth into a higher dimension will also increase the frequency of the entire universe, because we are one. Many ETI's or extraterrestrial Intelligences are aware of this and working towards an increased frequency in the oneness.

There have never been more sightings of UFO's than today. Aliens are all around and amongst us to help the human race. In the previous chapter about our connection with aliens we find convincing evidence of this. As mentioned before, there are also man made UFO's that are there to deceive you. We still live in that era of deception, but not for long any longer.

On a more scientific note, we know of the existence of spectrum peaks in the extremely low frequency part of our Earth's electromagnetic field spectrum called the Shumann

Resonance (SR). It was named after the man who discovered them. It consists of global electromagnetic resonances that are formed in the cavity of the Earth's surface and it's Ionosphere triggered by lightning discharges.

According to NASA the ionosphere is composed of a layer of electrons, Ionized atoms and molecules which stretches from approximately 30 miles above the Earth up to 600 miles (the edge of space). It is a highly flexible region that shrinks and expands. That region also makes our radio transmissions possible.

The reason why I mention this is because the electromagnetic resonances have an influence on all life on Earth. The signals are linked to our Earth's magnetic field. We learned about the law of vibration, which showed us that everything around us vibrates and circles including our own body. The Shumann Resonance is what harmonizes the pulse for life on Earth. It will influence our health and that of all life around us.

It is the heartbeat of Mother Earth, a harmonizing pulse for all life on Earth.

It was **Lewis B. Hainsworth,** who was amongst the first to suggest that our health and that of all living creatures is linked to a geophysical framework, which is occurring in a natural way in the extremely low frequencies. (Shumann ELF) It is setting the tempo for our well-being and health.

Hainsworth concluded in his study about the brainwave evolution that the frequencies of human brain-waves can be altered by the Shumann extremely low frequencies. This brings us to the observation and influence of the approaching Nibiru system, which has a huge electromagnetic field, clearly influencing all the planets in our solar system, including our own Sun. The approach of the Nibiru system triggered an important increase in solar flares, which in return influences the electromagnetic resonances of Earth.

Hainsworth stated that; *"As human beings we have extraordinary potentials we have hardly begun to study, much less understand. Creative gifts, intuition and talents that are unpredictable or emergent may become stabilized in generations to come. Hopefully, we can learn to understand both our emergence from an essentially electromagnetic environment and facilitate our potential for healing, growth and non-local communication."*

Our planet communicates with us via resonance. This is the reason why shamans use drums and trance dance to align with Earth's resonance. It is a form of harmonization with our planetary field, the opening of other dimensions and evidence that humans have synchronized with the planetary resonance since ancient times. It is most likely also the reason why being in nature is a healing experience for humans. Ancient Indian Rishis referred to it as *"Ohm"* , the purest sound or vibration, which is the tuning fork for life. Different type of healers are using techniques to align the body, mind and soul to the Shumann Resonance. Some call it energy medicine technology, in reality it's the ability to remove the constraints and limitations of the mind and connect with the greater "self" or the state of oneness. The state in which we are feeling one with the universe.

Author **Bradford Keeney** in his book; *"Everyday Soul:Awakening the Spirit in Daily life"*, will give you a deeper insight about the subject, for those of you who want to learn more about the matter. He will describe how you can consciously align yourself to the Shumann Resonance and be in a natural and harmonic relationship with Earth.

However; if we come back to our current situation, the interference of the Nibiru system will change our Shumann Resonances in a way we never experienced before. This will allow people to align much faster with the frequency of the Universe and become one with it.

There's much more to know about the Schumann Resonances in order to understand its importance and influence on our life and that of all living creatures on our Earth.

According to **Dr. Michael Persinger** of Laurentian University in Canada, the 7-8 Hz range of brainwave frequencies are linking the human brain to our Earth's geomagnetic field. Further research suggest that the Earth's magnetic field can act as a psychic information highway that can be linked to unexplained psychic phenomena. Dr. Persinger concluded; in his research on psychic communication and phenomena that there's a correlation between geomagnetic activity and psychic phenomena.

Researchers observed an important increase in the Shumann Resonances in recent years, as from 2014 the frequency rose from 7,83 Hz to 15,25 Hz and in January 2017 it recorded more than 36 Hz. It means that the level increased by fivefold in only a few years. What would cause this anomaly and will it affect people? It is a fact that the Schumann Resonances increased drastically when the Nibiru system entered our inner solar system.

Further research concluded that human consciousness can have an important impact on the Earth's magnetic field and vice versa. We live in a era of very high stress levels, political and economical instability, threat of war, terrorism, and all the elements that are contributing to our anxiety and tension on a worldwide scale. Would this be related to the important increase in frequency?

There is evidence that an increase in frequency will also increase our consciousness and level of awareness. This which in return would explain why so many people suddenly find themselves questioning some failing structures on political, religious as well as economical levels. Humanity is feeling incompatibilities in the old system, experiencing a new perception of opening awareness. Feelings of compassion and love are the soul's need when it reaches higher frequencies. The higher the frequencies, the more diversified information can be transmitted and the more we will be able to understand the universe and become one with it.

Do you have the perception that time is accelerating? Don't worry, many people are experiencing the same today. It just might be a result of the increase in the Earth's frequency. The acceleration of time is causing anxiety, confusion, chronic stress, fatigue and in some cases even nervous breakdowns. According to my own research; I conclude that we have two main reasons to why time is accelerating and what is happening to us:

1) On a scientific level; the Schumann Resonances are increasing significantly and by doing so also increasing the speed of time. A theory that was confirmed by Einstein, when he stated that time can speed up.

2) On a more spiritual level, the increase in frequencies is bringing us closer to a new dimension Spiritual growth that took years before, will now happen in a much shorter time period. Giving humanity a chance to step into a new realm or dimension. We are experiencing opportunities to pay off Karmic debts much faster in this life, which is only the result of an acceleration of events that help us change.

I am convinced that the violence, stress and turbulence that the world is undergoing now will slowly disappear as the frequencies will continue to increase. We arrived at a point of no return in the history of humanity and can only move forward and embrace our new spiritual awakening.

Signs that we are on the right path

The arrival of Nibiru in our inner solar system created a huge stream of information, disinformation by government, as well as fear mongering people just trying to make money out of this event. The focus of the media has been on the physical rather than the spiritual aspect. It is quite human to be afraid of what will happen to your physical presence on Earth when the Nibiru system is supposed to create havoc. It's making the spiritual side much more difficult and almost insignificant to comprehend. After all; this is exactly what the elite need, they want people to live in fear, as that is their means of control.

The elite are aware of the awakening of millions of people around the world, making it almost impossible to hide their plans, regardless of how hard they try, they can't hide it any longer. They're also conscious of the increase in Earth's vibrations, which will trigger an increased spiritual level, something the elite doesn't want to happen. As people move to a higher frequency, the material world of the elite as they created it today, the whole monetary system including the world economy will totally collapse, leaving them empty handed.

As Mother Earth is increasing her vibrational frequency with the help of the Nibiru system, we are also increasing our spiritual awareness exponentially. It is raising our consciousness to greater truth and understanding. As mentioned in the laws of the universe before, we also influence the Schumann Resonance by our mind. We have to understand that the human being is not just a body.

The human being is comprised of five bodies:

- The physical

- The emotional

- The mental

- The spiritual

- The higher self

Any change in Mother Earth's energy field will directly affect all the bodies mentioned above, as they will need a new alignment. This might be the reason why we experience an increase in strange feelings, such as depression, exhaustion and discomfort in general, beside other physical problems. It is our body trying to adapt to the new frequencies, some researchers called this phenomenon the "Ascension Syndrome."

Humanity is on one of the most important crossroads in its existence. It will be the choice between the technological and material world that is currently in the hands of the elite and that of a raised spiritual consciousness that is already ingrained in our DNA and part of what we are (a light being).

I am convinced that the violence, stress and turbulence that the world is undergoing now will slowly disappear as the frequencies will continue to increase. We arrived at a point of no return in the history of humanity and can only move forward and embrace our new spiritual awakening.

In a former chapter we discussed some points how we can find out if we are ready for the awakening. Now I will give some points that are proving that we're already experiencing an increased vibration and ready to enter the next dimension.

As always, in line with the principles of the universe, it will be a free choice for humanity.

Here under you will find some major signs indicating that your soul is already on a higher frequency and the highway to spiritual growth :

- A strongly increased intuition.

- You feel an important shift in your interest in media, movies and even music. You start seeing the truth amongst all the lies the media is feeding you.

- You have the feeling that you became an entirely different person.

- You can feel that time is accelerating.

- Your develop a sudden interest in mythical teachings, mysteries and spirituality.

- There is an overwhelming feeling of oneness with the Universe.

- You become very sensitive to negative energies

- The frequency of your dreams has increased

- Your love for nature, animals is higher than ever before

- Your body and mind start protesting when eating processed foods.

- Your immune system has increased, you will have less visits to the doctor.

- You don't feel like partying or going out any longer, you feel that there are other pleasures in life that are much more fulfilling.

- You feel more emotions of pure love

The elite are losing the battle

The more the elite are trying to control the world, the more entropy occurs, leaving the world in a state of total chaos. Here under you will find a number of reasons why they are losing the battle to control humanity.

Trust in politicians and governments is gone

The approval rating of politicians worldwide has fallen to an all time low. They're recognized as puppets of the elite by not serving the people that elected them as they should do in line with their respective mandates. Political trust is necessary to obtain democratic rule. This is a challenge to the elite representing the so called democracy, which became synonymous for controlling organism. Distrust is generated by a lack of procedural fairness, corruption and poor economic performance in regard to what was initially promised to the electorate.

The above mentioned neglects are probably playing a major factor, but there is more to it than just that. As people's awareness rises, so does the understanding they will obtain of the web of lies surrounding the global political agendas.

There is a strong movement of people trusting their peers more than any government leader, which is not serving the objectives of the elite. When trust in government is gone, confidence of investors and consumers will decrease. Many of the regulations are depending on cooperation and compliance of citizens. The lack of trust will ultimately lead to a collapse of the whole system as it exists today. Would that be bad? No, it would lead the way to a totally new form of government.

Trust in banks is gone

The consumer's trust in the banking system has gone. Different studies indicate that the four top banks in the world are the least loved brands. Peoples claims are that banks are too expensive and many of them think they will be redundant in the near future. There are signs that the end of the debt creators is in sight. The IMF has been rejected by Iceland, Hungary and the Russian Federation. Recent withdrawals from the IMF, World Bank and ICSID by Latin American governments is a clear sign that poorer and less powerful countries reject the conditions they impose, another awakening on a bigger scale. They clearly understood that they were seeking the privatization of public enterprises, reducing public employment and weakening protection for workers and unions.

All signs are there that the elite is implementing plans for total control. The founding fathers and brain behind the above mentioned international banking organizations.

The objective is clear; full control of the country's natural resources, privatize as much companies as possible, take over the country's incumbent telecommunications, electricity and water companies. All this by forcing them into a scheme of planned loans, which will ultimately force them into submission as they won't be able to reimburse their huge debts. The technique is simple, yet very efficient, force countries into debts and then establish or control the Central Bank in the country.

Recent studies indicate that money is the greatest source of anxiety for all age groups, although with a very high percentage for the youth. In a society that only worship money and the power that comes with it, people become victims of the banking system when society is forcing them into loans in order to keep up with the consumerists expectations. Fortunately, many people realize that having less material belongings doesn't mean that they will be less happy.

Less is more !

Lost confidence in the media

Recent polls suggest that more than 70% of the population no longer trusts corporate TV news and any other form of public media in general. News is not reported fully, accurately or fairly because they are controlled by people with a specific agenda, that of brainwashing the population.

The majority is aware of this phenomenon and are rather trusting their peers on social media than the official media channels. The link between the media and the elite controlling it, is no secret any longer. With our current Internet connection, news can be spread more efficiently and instantly via people in the region where the events are taking place. That is the reason why more and more people are turning to the Internet for unbiased news (Although there is a lot of fake news too).

The main reason for the lost trust in the media is directly linked to the global awakening of us all, a craving for the truth and an increased intuition for lies. Our augmented ability to see the truth behind the lies and the relentless influencing of the public opinion in order to reach their objectives is part of the awakening process.

The mainstream media, composed by giant media conglomerates are reluctant to investigate and certainly to comment on government policies, intelligence, defense and all other security related issues. Coverage about the destruction of the twin towers of the World Trade Center on September 11 in 2001, the wars in Afghanistan and Iraq, the constant Muslim threat from Al Qaeda up to the recent ISIS threat, all to create a false reality. Fortunately, thanks to the awakening, people can see through the deception.

Governments lies disclosed

The time that governments can feed any information as real to the public is over. People are not taking for granted all the disinformation they spread to serve a single agenda, that of the elite. Today we are surrounded by fake news and even more alternative facts that are far from the truth, yet it is spread by governments.

In recent times, new information about global surveillance and government secrecy emerged and was distributed and disclosed by Wikileaks, Edward Snowden (NSA whistleblower) and many others in the past. All those people experienced an increased state of awareness and justice, which pushed them to the disclosure of often highly sensitive governmental and military unlawful practices to the public.

New evidence of governmental fraud was disclosed in the 90s, but there has never been more disclosures than today, whistleblowers are coming out of the woodwork and governments are seriously struggling to keep scandals contained.

In 1996 the San Jose Mercury News published a series of articles under the name *"Dark Alliance"* , written by Gary Webb. They disclosed that the CIA was turning a blind eye when Nicaraguan drug traffickers distributed crack cocaine in Los Angeles in the 80s. In the same article the writer disclosed that the Reagan administration protected known drug dealers from prosecution.

The list of whistleblowers is long; Watergate (FBI agent Mark Felt), The Pentagon Papers (Daniel Ellsberg), Trailblazer (Thomas Drake), Coleen Rowley (FBI), Bradley Manning (United States Army), Russell Tice (National Security Agency), and Edward Snowden (National Security Agency), just to mention a few.

Our awakening consciousness doesn't allow injustice and lies any longer.

Vatican in discredit

Scandals ranging from money laundry and fraud to a multitude of reported pedophile priests are bringing the real values of the church down. The credibility of the church has taken a big blow and people are standing up to reveal or know the truth. The Vatican faces a lack of unity and trust, created by recently disclosed information to the public. The recent sexual offense allegations against Cardinal George Pell have immersed the Vatican in an even deeper crisis. As the third most powerful figure in the church, many people were shocked by the allegations.

The Pope himself is being accused and convicted of crimes. There is a profound reason why people don't go to church any longer. Thousands of churches are closing their doors every year around the world and there is no end to that movement. Understandably clergy abuse cases, the cover-up by the church of wrongdoing and fundamental preachers are driving people away from church. Recent evidence from leaked Vatican secret documents revealed that the church is involved in what is called the "Magisterial Privilege" compelling the participation of every new elected Pope in the "Ninth Circle" sacrifice of newborn children.

Most people are more aware of the atrocities committed by the church during the Dark Ages, when millions of people were slaughtered because they didn't worship God as imposed by the church. The papacy claimed it had the right to slaughter "heretics" (which is still true today). The question raised by the author is; heretics of what kind of religion?

It is clear that the Church of Rome has shed more innocent blood than any other institution. According to Kevin Annett (Canadian whistleblower and Nobel Prize Nominee), of the **International Tribunal into Crimes of Church and State (ITCCS),** five judges and 27 jury members from six countries, including the USA, considered evidence on over 50,000 children, suspected victims of an international child sacrificial cult; "the Ninth Circle" (Source ITCCS.ORG).

At a Brussels (Belgium) Common Law Court of Justice; two adolescent woman claimed that Pope Francis raped them while participating in a child sacrifice (Source whale.to in an article of Judy Byington). Sealed Vatican documents, exposed by remorseful insiders, revealed horrible Satanic rituals. On August 4, 2013, the same court in Brussels issued a legal declaration, naming the Crown of England and the Roman Catholic Church as Transnational Criminal bodies under International law. The International Tribunal into Crimes of Church and State mentioned in a report that; *"Along with considerable documentation, the Prosecutor introduced notarized affidavit statements from eight eyewitnesses to these crimes, including videotaped interviews with two adolescent woman who claim to have been tortured and raped by chief defendant Jorge Bergoglio, alias "Pope Francis", during the spring of 2009 and 2010, at horrific cult functions connected to the "Ninth Circle" child sacrifice network."*

The Chief Prosecutor to the Court described that witnesses revealed the fact that newborn babies were chopped to pieces on stone altars, after which the remains would be consumed by the participants. I can understand that the reader will be reluctant to accept these reports, changing our complete view on the Vatican and what this organization has represented for centuries. I was baptized and raised Catholic, went to a Catholic boarding school and believe me, I was shocked when I discovered the above allegations. I cross checked the allegations, but unfortunately they seem to be genuine and sincere.

In accordance to records of the ITCCS, The "Ninth Circle" was established by the Jesuits in 1773 and three years later part of the Illuminati cult. There is further evidence that organized child sacrifice rituals were done at Catholic cathedrals in Rome as from 1528.

Disclosed Jesuit documents confirm the existence of yet another child sacrificial cult named "The Knights of Darkness", which was established by Nazi Waffen S.S. Division with the support of the Jesuits. Former Pope Benedict (Joseph Ratzinger), was a member of this organization and it is known that he participated in sacrificial rites using children from political prisoners when he was an S.S.Chaplain's assistant at the Ravensbruck concentration camp in Germany.

The writer is not pointing at each priest or member of organizations like the Freemasons. I have friends amongst them and they are most often not aware of the activities and hidden objectives of their leaders. It is time to wake up and I can see that it is happening all around us.

Their evil rule is over! For those still hesitating; Is it the love of God they praise...or that of the Antichrist? You are the judge.

Secession movements around the world

Several European countries are trying to get out of the EU. The UK has already made the decisions, others might follow. We see national secession movements within countries too, like the ones in Scotland, Spain, Belgium, France and many other countries. In America, secession movements are increasing too, specifically in California and Colorado.

Globalization could be the reason behind the increased secession movements around the world. If globalization would effectively intensify the social and cultural interconnectedness, it would be perceived differently than it appeal to people today. Trust of intergovernmental organizations, such as the United Nations (UN) and nongovernmental organizations (NGO's) is completely lost.

The reason why secession claims are increasing around the world can be found in the awakening of the collective mind. The understanding that only a total separation with a formal withdrawal from an established, internationally recognized state can stop the globalization program that was planned, and soon in the final completion phase by the elite. It indicates again that humanity is in a state of awakening.

The rejection of GMO food

People don't accept the pesticide-soaked and manipulated food any longer, despite the huge efforts of multinationals like BASF, Bayer, DuPont, Monsanto, Syngenta and Dow Chemical Company, just to mention the 6 most important companies involved, to market them.

The amount of genetically engineered crops grown around the world is decreasing in terms of acreage whereas the organic sector is growing. Scientists are starting to realize that the GMO technology is failing as super-pests and super-weeds are developing around the world and hampering their efforts to manipulate nature. It is clearly Mother Earth's answer to what they try to achieve. Consumers around the world are aware of the toxic herbicides and pesticides used on them and therefore refuse to buy or consume them.

I mentioned this subject to show that there must be a balance in order to have a clean and sustainable world. That balance should be found and is always available within nature itself, not by trying to alter it.

A New world, not a New World Order

Will there be a New World Order after predicted cataclysmic events on Earth ?

Scientists argue that only earthquakes could result in a pole shift are unlikely, but asteroids impact would be the most probable cause of the shift, as it happened many times before. A strong magnetic pull from the Nibiru system could give a final push.

Could this be the reason why the elite are building underground facilities and at the same time buying property far away from the coastlines? Not just any property or location, the carefully selected locations are ideal for farming and creating a self-sustainable life. Isn't the sudden interest of the elite in farming and cattle a sign that they know their survival will depend on it?

Elizabeth Stamp, a writer for CNN reported in her article *"Billionaire bunkers: How the 1% are preparing for the apocalypse"*, that an important number of specialized companies in bunkers have an extraordinary increase in demand the last years. She mentioned that *"the world's elite, including hedge fund managers , sports stars and tech executives (Bill Gates is rumored to have bunkers at all his properties) have chosen to design their own secret shelters to house their families and staff."* Gary Lynch (general manager of Texas based Rising S company), claimed that sales between 2015 and 2016 were up by 700% .

The Doomsday demand, as they call it, showing an out of proportion increase in sales of underground bunkers, made a lot of "common people" think about what they would know that we don't. Are they preparing for World War III, a nuclear attack, an asteroid impact, a Pole shift, or even a combination of different elements?

There are many ideas and opinions to what will really happen and when the supposed pole shift will occur. It was the futurist and teacher of consciousness studies and spiritual visionary **Gordon-Michael Scallion,** who claimed to have had a spiritual awakening in the 80's and saw in great detail the map of a new world, the one after the pole shift. He believed that the cause for it would be global warming and misuse of nuclear power. He predicted a 20 to 40 degree shift.

The cataclysmic change triggered by the pole shift could lead to what Scallion saw in his spiritual inspired dream. For readers interested in the future maps, I refer to an article by **Jim Dobson** " *The shocking Doomsday Map of The World And The Billionaires Escape Plans* ", in Forbes.com.

According to leading scientific teams from major research centers around the world, axis shifts have only occurred every few million, even billion years and take millions of year to complete. We do observe an important wobble of Earth today, but how often this occurred in the past is unclear to scientists. The incoming Nibiru system is certainly playing a major role into this event.

Edgar Casey (famous psychic and theorist), predicted that the shift would take a very long time. Casey said that we will see a change in our Pole star, from Polaris to Vegas. The ancient Egyptians noticed this event and called it "Thuban", it marked the move into a new era.

Regarding this event Casey said that "*This indicates it is the system towards which the soul takes it flight after having completed its sojourn through the solar system. The Dipper is gradually changing, and when this change becomes noticeable – as might be calculated from the Pyramid – there will be the beginning of the change in the races (root races, not color races). There will come a greater influx of souls from the Atlantean, Lemurian, La, Ur, or Da civilizations.*"

It is clear that we are entering into a New Age. Regarding this shift Casey replied the following to the question what it would mean to humanity;

"The full consciousness of the ability to communicate with the Creative Forces and be aware of the relationship to the Creative Forces and the uses of same in material environs. This awareness during the era or Age of Atlantis and Lemuria or Mu brought what? Destruction of man and his beginning of the needs of the journey up through that of selfishness" (Edgar Casey reading 1602-3)

As we saw earlier in the law of polarity, our world is composed of opposite thoughts and actions. Some of the current most relevant opposites:

- Humanity is destroying Earth - humanity is saving Earth

- People are asleep – people are awake

- People want war – people want peace

When we look around us, we can clearly notice that there are different approaches in our current world, we can divide them in two distinctive groups. There is a world in which the elite is trying to impose materialism and an egocentric society (New World Order), a place where millions of people will serve only a few and another world with millions of people awakening, realizing that the only way forward is to increase our consciousness level to a higher frequency and by doing so, embracing love and compassion as the new world's *modus vivendi*. We are not alone in this transition into a new dimension. As the latter is considered as a major event in the universe, we are assisted by many spiritual beings, residing on earth, around Earth and on the different planes in the universe.

This might appears to come straight out of a science fiction movie, but there is convincing evidence that we are surrounded by aliens that are helping us. Alien civilizations are monitoring our planet's polar axes and magnetic field and have the technology to smooth the ride when it happens. They are doing this for all the planets in the universe, because astrophysical and geophysical conditions affecting earth, are also affecting the whole interconnected grid of the universe.

The final message of my spiritual guide who motivated me to write this book, is not to be afraid of what is coming, despite all the doom scenarios. We need to keep a positive mindset and focus on the beautiful future ahead. The spiritual expansion of consciousness will allow us to have a much greater understanding of the divine functions of the universe and our ability to interact with it.

The elite will be sitting in their bunkers trying to survive the destruction of a material world of which they desire full control. The reality however; is that they will be left behind while millions of people will make the move into the new dimension.

As the book of revelations and so many other ancient scriptures predicted, the shift will also encompass the so long desired return of the Christ. Don't be fooled by the false coming as described before, it will only be a distraction of the real coming, which will be felt in the heart and soul, without any need of visual holographic projections.

The main force of the universe is love, no other frequency is higher and will be able to replace it. Therefore; it's the main reason why the "New World Order" creation by the elite will **fail.** They can't feel love and compassion, and this will be their end. A "New World" of enlightened people has already been created and just waiting for new souls to join them. We only have to change our frequency in order to see and experience it.

Conclusion

By expecting a New World Order, the Antichrist and the predicted apocalypse, we are feeding the collective consciousness of the "dark energy", this is exactly what they want us to do. The elite are playing the "fear-card" to lower the increasing frequencies that make people more aware and initiate their ascent to spirituality. It is the biggest threat to the implementation of the New World Order.

Rather than being afraid of our future, we should embrace it by looking into the new dimension and expect miracles, creating the Golden Age. When the mass consciousness moves into that direction, which it is already doing right now, the elite's New World Order will completely collapse...and they are well aware of it.

What is described as "The heavens" by the Bible is nothing other than our parallel spiritual world. What we will experience very soon is the awareness that we live in a multi-dimensional universe. For the moment; most people can only see three dimensions within our physical time and space, but we slowly become aware of the fact that the spiritual dimensions consist of many more other dimensions of reality.

As we live in a material world, most people can only believe in what is visible or proven by science. The biggest change humanity is experiencing now is the growing understanding that our physical world is linked to a spiritual world and that both worlds are interconnected and influence all aspects of our life. The multi-dimensional universe contains both the physical and spiritual dimensions or realms.

As directed by the laws of the universe, we have the law of mind over matter, which is the opposite of what we experience on Earth today. Once we understand our true spiritual powers, there is nothing we can't realize in life.

The forces behind the elite are also using spiritual power to achieve their objectives, although they are using the low frequencies of dark spiritual forces. (hence multiple accounts of ritual sacrifices). They were able to use this power over a very long period of time, allowing them to create their kingdom on Earth.

When people talk about the coming of the Antichrist, I have to disagree, there is no coming, he is already in power since a very long time on Earth. The only change might be that we will finally understand that he is amongst us and see it with our own new opened spiritual eyes.

The battle that is raging for the moment is an important **spiritual** battle that reflects on our physical world or realm, creating the chaos we see all around us. One could compare it as the final battle of good against evil, a battle in which evil will be expelled from Earth soon.

The Nibiru system, although seen as a doomsday player by many, should rather be seen as the arrival of God to our rescue. He will be assisted by light beings and advanced alien civilizations. By increasing the Schumann Resonances (to use some scientific facts discussed in this book), our spiritual awareness and global consciousness will increase to a level in which we can move into another higher dimension, leaving the elite in the present-day third dimension behind.

The current boundary between the physical and spiritual realm will disappear, opening a completely New World for us. It will NOT be the New World Order conceived by dark Spiritual forces, but a world of peace, stability, harmony and prosperity.

The Spiritual awakening of the people is the most powerful resistance against all the values the elite represent today. The highest frequency in the universe is love, annihilating all the others.

The anxiety created by of our society is the reason why people often generate low vibrations, making them sick or at least developing health problems. When you change your mindset to love, joy, gratitude and compassion your vibrations will increase and you will feel much better. Humans have the ability to self heal, but they forgot all about it in the material world.

I come again to one of my most important points, we create what we think, so we have the choice to create our new world just by visualizing it. The power of the mind has no limits !

I wish you all the best on this amazing voyage to your new dimension, Love.

Bibliography

Baron Eugene Fersen ; *"The Science of being"*

Bradford Keeney ; *"Everyday Soul:Awakening the Spirit in Daily life"*

C.Wright Mills; "The Power Elite"

David Meade; *"Will Planet X signal the rapture"*

Dr. Bernard Eastlund; *"the largest ionosphere heater ever built"* (article)

Dr. Michael Persinger; *"research on psychic communication and phenomena"*

Dr. Stephen D. Mumford; *"American Democracy and The Vatican: Population Growth and National Security"*

Erich von Daniken; *"Chariots of the Gods?*

Elizabeth Stamp; *"Billionaire bunkers: How the 1% are preparing for the apocalypse"* (CNN article)

Jim Dobson; *"The shocking Doomsday Map of The World And The Billionaires Escape Plans "* in Forbes.com (Article)

Jean-Guy Vaillancourt; *"Papal Power; a study of Vatican Control over Lay Catholic elites*

Jim Green; (NASA), Article: *"Hypothetical 'Planet X': overview"*

Lewis B. Hainsworth; "the brainwave Evolution"

Socioecohistory.wordpress.com; "the council of 13"

Mary M. Davison; *"The Profound Revolution"*

Mark Elkin; *"Hidden Knowledge – unravelling the pole shift"* and *"New Earth"* Facebook research and survival group

Marc Gielissen; *"Roots in the Congo"*

Nikola Tesla; *"My inventions: The autobiography of Nikola Tesla"*

Piers Compton; *"The Broken Cross"*

Paul Watson; "Order out of Chaos – Elite Sponsored Terrorism & the New World Order"

Serge Monast; *"Project Blue Beam (NASA)"*

Stanley Milgram; *"Research paper on obedience and authority"*

Pat Robertson; *"The New World Order"*

WikiLeaks; *"The Email for John Podesta re Disclosure"*

Wikipedia; *"New World Order"*